The Celts – A Deep Look

The Celtic People, and Their Way of Life

D1799116

Introduction – About the Book

I want to personally thank you, and congratulate you for obtaining the book "*The Celts - A Deep Look: The Celtic People, and Their Way of Life*"

This book is a short summary of the history of the Celtic people, their language, religion, and culture. While it isn't a complete textbook on the life and culture of the Celts, it is a quick in-depth look at them designed to dissuade any stereotypes that persist about them as a people. This book is also designed to help be used as a starting point for any sort of in-depth study.

What you'll find inside is a basic run down of their rise, from how they united as a sort of tribe and spread out from the Bronze Age to dominate much of Continental Europe, making their way successfully all the way to the British Isles before their fall to other, later civilizations such as the Germanic Tribes, Rome, and other Tribal people. You'll also find within descriptions about what their daily lives were like, how their society subsisted and grew, as well as how they fought hard, worked hard, worshiped hard, and lived. Not only that, but you'll also read a small comprehensive guide to their religion as well, all to better understand how these people were.

Thank you again for choosing this book. A lot of time researching, and a lot of love crafting it, and a lot of talented writing went into its creation all for your reading pleasure. Hope you enjoy!

© **Copyright 2016 by Ray Abel All rights reserved.**

This document is geared towards providing exact and reliable information in regards to the topic and issue covered. The publication is sold with the idea that the publisher is not required to render accounting, officially permitted, or otherwise, qualified services. If advice is necessary, legal or professional, a practiced individual in the profession should be ordered.

- From a Declaration of Principles which was accepted and approved equally by a Committee of the American Bar Association and a Committee of Publishers and Associations.

In no way is it legal to reproduce, duplicate, or transmit any part of this document in either electronic means or in printed format. Recording of this publication is strictly prohibited and any storage of this document is not allowed unless with written permission from the publisher. All rights reserved.

The information provided herein is stated to be truthful and consistent, in that any liability, in terms of inattention or otherwise, by any usage or abuse of any policies, processes, or directions contained within is the solitary and utter responsibility of the recipient reader. Under no circumstances will any legal responsibility or blame be held against the publisher for any reparation, damages, or monetary loss due to the information herein, either directly or indirectly.

Respective authors own all copyrights not held by the publisher.

The information herein is offered for informational purposes solely, and is universal as so. The presentation of the information is without contract or any type of guarantee assurance.

The trademarks that are used are without any consent, and the publication of the trademark is without permission or backing by the trademark owner. All trademarks and brands within this book are for clarifying purposes only and are the owned by the owners themselves, not affiliated with this document.

Contents

Chapter 1 – The Rise of the Great Celts

The history of who we call Celts is difficult to piece together. Firstly, their own history was never written, as was the case in BC cultures. And secondly, they were more like a handful of tribes that shared little other than some aspects of culture and language. So, most of what we know about them today is through the efforts of historians and archaeologists digging around the archives of Ancient Greeks and Romans.

Celts start coming up in ancient writings about 1200-500 BC. Contrary to what we may think, they did not originate in the British Isles nor Italy. In fact, precisely because they were so fragmented, they spread out to (what we know today as) Italy, France, Austria, Germany, Hungary, Great Britain, Ireland, Spain, Portugal, the Czech Republic, Greece, Switzerland, Slovakia, and even Turkey. The reason for the large gap in time and the plethora of regions that the Celtic influence was found in was, again, because of how spread out they were. The only ways to really track their movements were to follow their art styles, burial traditions (even though each tribe had their own variations and deities they believed in), the writings of their neighbors, and archaeological remains. The former was largely influenced by the cultures they were near to, namely the Greeks and the Romans. The evolution in their art marked a new chapter in their reign. As skilled blacksmiths of the Iron Age, they took up on the task of becoming superior artists in Classical Age; however, not only in the art as we understand it, but the art of war, as well.

The Celts were never peaceful people, resorting to expansionism by force. They were not considered barbarians by the Romans for nothing, after all. After being defeated and pushed back by Eastern Europeans, they instead marched south, sacking Rome, Greece, and later Turkey. Soon after – France, Great Britain, and everything else on their way.

Chapter 2 – The Fall of the Celts

The biggest problem with the Celtic "Empire" was that it never was one. They were always fragmented, never had a single leader, or a unified plan of action. They achieved much, but rarely as "they". This was always to be their downfall.

Never growing out of the wanderer mindset, various tribes began to move around as soon as 300 BC. With no clear idea of where they are going, they simply packed up and picked a direction. Some more agricultural types found their place in random points on the map and eventually assimilated into the cultures, the more ferocious types went to war with Greece, Rome, or Germany, others became mercenaries and fought for whoever paid the most, still others fought amongst themselves and declared war on other Celtic tribes. Eventually, the only few cohesive Celtic regions that were still left were Great Britain and Gaul.

Being such a nuisance to the Romans, it did not take long for the Celts to paint a target on their back. They were an especially big target to Caius Julius Caesar, who was not the leader of Rome at the time, but was on his way to becoming a warlord to be feared. Thus, enter the Gallic Wars.

The division between Celts was once more a problem for them. This was where the famous "divide and conquer" line came from. As some Celtic tribes were at war with each other, they were more than happy to lend a hand to the Romans to take their enemies down, which soon turned around to bite back. 8 years later, the only Celtic-controlled area left was Great Britain.

In 42 AD, emperor Claudius of the Roman Empire invaded Britain with the intent of finishing what Caesar started. He took a similar strategy by turning the tribes against one another and using it to his advantage. It did not take long to annihilate most of the tribes; however, the Scots, western Britain and Ireland remained, the former of which terrorized the south at any given opportunity. It is thanks to the druids who survived and recorded their knowledge of Celtic culture that we know so much of what we can only say is a collection of Celts (and not an empire).

Chapter 3 – The Celtic Military

"The Celts were fearless warriors because they wish to inculcate this as one of their leading tenets. Those souls do not become extinct, but pass after death from one body to another."

-Julius Caesar

Make no mistake. The Celts were a very hard people. While they were predominately a farming society, and they tended to live peacefully in villages that were called Homesteads, they were often very hard, and very brutal with one another, especially through the use of the Clan system that dominated their culture.

Tribal warfare was often and very common, and was used as a tool from other Homesteads and clans to gather much-needed resources and territory from competing Clans and Homestead, as well as used as an intimidation tactic against perceived weaker opponents or to gain economic advantages. While the goal of Tribal warfare wasn't ever the total annihilation of their opponents, and was used more as a tool to raid, hunt, and used as a sport, to say that it was bloodless is a vast understatement.

Militarily the Celts also never had a true standing army either, which was a disadvantage that their contemporaries were quick to take advantage of whenever they could. The Nordic and Germanic were competitors, but fared much in the same way as they did as they weren't centralized, but instead tribal based, but the Celts were easily overwhelmed and taken advantage of with their Roman counterparts, whose professional military easily outmaneuvered, and outfought the Celts unless numbers and terrain were on the Celts side.

Still, Celtic military life was dominated by the ideal of honor and bravery, much as any other Warrior culture that existed throughout human history. They believed less in the ideas of tactics however and believed fully that a warrior's duty was to bring honor to him, and his clan above all else, and to protect what they had.

Weapons and Armor

Being around during the Bronze and Iron Ages had its benefits, and the Celts were famous for reaping those benefits. They were incredible blacksmiths and it showed in their battles. For armor, they began with cloth and leather but later moved on to bronze plates. They also invented the chainmail, but they were also known for sewing metal plates onto cloth armor, thus combining the defensive power of cloth and metal. Helmets were not too popular at the beginning, but there are some sources that say they eventually had similar helmets to those of the Romans, but it is not certain who copied who. When the Celts did wear helmets, they were often decorated and even had metal horns to make them look taller. For a shield, the Celts had large oval or rectangle -shaped slabs of wood or metal, often having a metal part in the middle to catch the opponents' weapons and could be used for ramming and bashing.

For weapons, the Celts had two favorites – spears and swords. There were two types of spears that they used a light one that could be thrown and a heavier one made for use on the battlefield. Swords started off as relatively short, more like the Romans', but eventually grew longer and sharper, even becoming dual-wielded by the Irish. Bows and slings were not a rarity, but the Celts seemed to prefer closer combat.

HORSES AND CHARIOTS. Few Celts actually rode on horseback, but instead, they were used in chariots. Chariots had several roles during combat. First, they served as vehicles to move a handful of the best warriors around. That way, it was easy to pick up a champion and move him to an area that needs him the most. Second, they served as another warrior, as the driver of the chariot would often use long-distance weapons, like throwing spears, while driving or as a defense for the champion coming on board. Finally, they were an intimidation factor. There is little else that scared warriors than being trampled by a horse, and the Celtic charioteers knew this, which is why they made the effort to appear loud and dangerous. This was helped by the fact that they were extremely agile on any type of terrain.

Cavalry appeared much later in the Celtic timeline and was mainly reserved for the upper classes. As is typical for cavalry, the main weapons were swords, but they often unleashed a flurry of spears at the enemy before finishing them off close with a sword.

Tactics

The Celtic tactic was much different from the tactics used by enemies outside of Celtic circles. As opposed to the careful and defense prone Romans, who they famously fought against time and time again, the Celts were typically went into battle strong, and hard, and believed fully in being able to overpower, overwhelm, and crush their enemies, often to the idea of just one command above all else: *Charge*!

In fact, the Celts were described by contemporary historians of the time as having fought like "Wild Beasts", choosing to fight using Horde based tactics in an almost literal frenzy that was often erratic, lacking in tactics, and very chaotic. In fact, military tacticians during the Roman era often reported having had to fight Celts differently from one day to next, as one moment they'd raise their swords and weapons and charge at them, attempting to drive back the legions, and the next moment they'd retreat to the forests that they came from and use guerrilla tactics to keep them on their toes and break up phalanx formations. It wasn't even uncommon for the Celts to eschew honorable tactics and instead conduct night raids on enemy encampments when most of the soldiers and warriors were supposed to be asleep, or even ambushed marching soldiers as they walked through the forests.

Of course, because of the changing times, and Roman intervention, even the Celts were no strangers to change as over time they developed their own tactics, often fighting dirty, and even taking up the tactics of their enemies. Eventually, the Celts developed other defensive minded tactics, such as developing their own version of a shield wall, and using the terrain to their advantage as well as developing pike formations to defeat and undermine cavalry attacks against their flanks. Often to the dismay of their enemies who expected them to be no more than dirty, naked savages.

The Warrior Mindset

As we've seen, the Celts were very strong warriors by nature and knew fully well that intimidation and psychologically torturing your enemies were a very big, and very real strength that they had over their enemies. In fact, this is how they operated, and often paid careful attention to not only who they fought, but how they fought as well.

This, of course, created a fierce reputation with the Celts and is actually where many of the stereotypes we have today come from. Unlike the Romans, who fought in tight formation with one another, wore armor, wielded various different weapons depending on the situation and were for the most part professional soldiers, Celtic warriors were much different. In fact Roman soldiers, and historians who saw the Celts fight first hand reported that they fought viciously, like wild animals and the legend of Celts fighting naked grew, often stating the Celts believed fully that if they fought naked, covered in a holy paint called Woad that turned their skin blue, and inscribed with prayers to their Gods that they'd be invincible in battle.

This led as well to the growing reputation of the Celts as a culture of Warriors who hunted heads, and it wasn't uncommon for Celtic warriors after a victory to cut off the head of famous, powerful warriors to display, believing fully that the soul of a person resided in the head. By "owning" their opponents head, they own their soul and was a way of achieving dominance over them. Head hunting became so widespread that after major battles with the Romans it wasn't uncommon to see rows of head dangling off of the side of horses, or even on the belts of woad-painted Warriors.

All of this combined paints a very striking, vicious image of the Celts that has lasted through generations, up until the modern time. While this Warrior mindset is still debated today, the truth of the Celts and their culture are rich and diverse, despite the truth of them being some of the most powerful warriors of their time.

Chapter 4 – Celtic Society, Language, and Culture

"Longer-lasting than any other thing is shame (buaine na gach nì an nàire)"

- Celtic proverb.

Celtic society was actually quite varied. The usual stereotype that many people have of the Celtic people are that they were savages who lived in the woods, possibly naked, covered in war paint and constantly on the prowl for victims to feed to their heathen gods. Of course, that's just a bunch of silly propaganda that started with the Romans, developed further with the Anglo-Saxons of Britain, and a Hollywood-ized view taken today of the Celts through film media.

In truth, they were both paradoxically different, yet similar all throughout. In fact, because of the widespread Culture of the Celts into mainland Europe, their society was distinctly different between Gaelic, Gaulic, Brittany, and Welsh people. Despite being a Late Bronze/Early Iron age people their society ranged in different social structures from between basic proto-feudalism where a King or Noble sat at the time, to a basic democratic system in some societies where all adult members of a Clan or Village had the right to put to a vote any decision.

However, for the most part throughout all of Celtic lands and culture, they subsisted mostly through a basic system of proto-feudalism that came to dominate much of European culture for centuries.

Societal Structure

The Celts had a pretty similar social structure to those of other cultures of the Iron/Classical Ages. The heads of the tribes were either king, who were thought to be the gods' representative, or magistrates, who were appointed by the nobility. In the first case, kings could nominate their successors and the position was rarely inherited. The second case was similar, but the actual magistrates were not so much in charge as served as a unified ruler that represented the interests of the nobility, a position, which was inheritable.

Commoners could always make a fortune from commerce or war as status was not inherited. Peasants with no money could go to nobility and serve, which earned them money at no cost to their rights. In fact, nobles had to protect their servants in cases of danger, which the servants repaid with loyalty and hard work.

The slaves were an interesting point for Celts. They were usually captives from war times and had no rights. However, if a nobleman freed them, they could become their servant, thus escaping the stigma.

Another layer of society was spirituality: the vates (prophets), druids, and bards. They were considered apart from the struggles of simple men, and highly esteemed. Traditions and lore permeated the lives of the Celts and vates, druids, and bards were the paragons of lore. Vates and druids represented the gods' relationship with humans, and bards spoke of history in music and poetry. It may seem strange that such a barbaric and war-loving culture could be so much in tune with spirituality, but the fact that there are still modern druids points to the impact they had during their time.

Language

For the most part, there is Archeological evidence that a lot of Celtic people spoke similarly, at the least in the early years of the Celtic people. While early on in the Bronze Age their language and culture started to spread from Continental Europe at a quick rate, spreading all the way towards the border of Eurasia, all the way across the small channel to the British Isles where they settled in Wales, and Ireland, and small pockets of Scotland. During this expansion they spoke a sort of language that Archeologists call a "Proto-Celtic Language" which wasn't based on the Latin alphabet (which itself was derived from Greek lettering), but instead was based off of runic writing that was pretty much built similarly like the Nordic language, which is believed to mean that they share some sort of common ancestry.

Still, one of the earliest records of a Proto-Celtic language comes from the Late Bronze Age in the Gaulic reason of Northern Italy, which was a language that was spoken in the area until the Roman Conquest during the early days of the Roman Expansion era around 300 B.C - 200 B.C.

However, with expansion and specialization comes differing languages throughout the years. While most of Continental Europe spoke a form of insular Celtic for centuries, those Celts who settled on the Irish-Welsh islands of Britain spoke a form of Primitive Irish known as "Irish Ogham Inscription" before fully forming into Gaelic in later centuries.

Architecture

The Celtic architecture was much different than what we imagine buildings to be like from the era that they thrived. While a lot of popular stereotypes exist of what life was like for the Celts, the truth of the matter was they lived very spartan lives, and their homes reflected it. They didn't have wooden homes, and stone forts, and massive sprawling towns where everyone lived close and side by side together with walls. Those were mostly architectural choices that didn't see much use until the Roman Conquest of Europe, the Dark Ages, and the Middle Ages afterward.

Instead, Wooden, and even Stone, buildings were kept for very important structures. The average Celtic peasant lived instead in a building that was called a "Roundhouse", which was several buildings that a family shared that was stitched together into a large structure made of mud brick walls, and straw or thatched roofing. Doors and Windows were cut open into the side of these buildings to allow for ventilation, but predominately these buildings were designed to be built up quickly, efficiently, and to protect members of the household against the elementals, especially during times of inclement weather.

However, the inside of these Roundhouses weren't built for more than sleeping or seeking shelter in. Predominantly outside of the home, often attached to outdoor facing walls were various different outbuildings that they used for various different reasons, also made of mud bricks, with straw, thatched, or needling roof above. Often these were left out in the open, as most of the time, these outbuildings were used to cook food, tan leather, smithy their weapons or more. Sometimes though they were enclosed buildings designed to store food or shelter animals. The unique characteristic of these outbuildings though was that they did not belong to any one member of the village. They belonged to everyone who needed them, and could work with them. This, of course, was all made possible by the fact that villages more or less were farming communities, as Celtic cities were very rare, so the population remained generally stable.

Still, that didn't mean they didn't on occasion build defensive structures. While the villages themselves were outlined with farms and fields outlying around the Roundhouses and Outbuildings, built away from the major areas where the people lived, they had two different levels of defense in case of attacks or danger.

The first major defense that was built was a small, waist-high wall of stone and stakes built around their territory on the very edge of the boundaries they lived at. Usually, this was no more than several feet high, only a foot or so thick and generally just acted as a deterrent to animals or other forest creatures. Often the outlying wall also was marked with various different religious symbols and offered places of offering for the Celts to offer food and other offerings to spiritual creatures, such as Elves, Trolls, or other fae folk, or to Gods and Goddesses.

However, in times of strife and warfare through inter-clan fighting, and later the Romans, the walls proved a poor defensive marker and more often than not were simply destroyed in the process of fighting.

So to combat human threats from other tribes, clans, and the Romans, the Celts devised an early form of castle and fort building called a Hill Fort. Usually, as the name implied, the hillfort was built on top of a Hill that was close to the villages and enclosed either with another ring of stone walls, or stakes in a palisade form. Eventually, the Celts even developed a way to create moats that surrounded the hills and acted as deterrents for sieges.

The Hilltop forts themselves weren't much better than the forts that would be developed later, but they sufficed in the area and time they were needed. Often these were the only wooden structures that the Celts built, and they were only built to be of a size big enough to accommodate the entire village with enough space to also accommodate farm animals and storage for food for several seasons. Their typical design was a major building in the center, often a tower, with huts and other roundhouses being built on the ground level, surrounded by tall wooden walls that acted as barriers from arrows and other projectiles from down below the hill. A large gateway was erected on one side, facing the gentlest sloping side of the hill to allow for ease of access in case of attack.

Art

Make no mistake, the Celts were viewed as a savage, hostile group of farmers and warriors to a lot of people outside of their circle, but their culture was still rich in artistic expression. Most archeologists and Art Historians who speak of Celtic Artwork typically speak of the type of art that was designed and adopted in an era known as the "La Tene Period and is usually called "insular art" in a historical context. Celtic artwork generally was pretty simple in appearance, but complex in design, and was heavily influenced by neighboring cultures before ultimately becoming absorbed into the Celtic culture itself.

One of the biggest influences of Celtic artwork still seen today is the "Celtic Knotwork" that is often seen and derived from the earliest parts of the Celtic culture and is a prime example of the sort of art that the Celts typically used. Instead of creating figures and artwork that was derived from figurative and imaginative points of views, such as statues, portraits, and the like, Celts typically created artwork that was heavily stylized and influenced by geometric shapes that were all interconnected altogether. Most of the time their artwork was heavily derived using energetic circular forms, spirals, triangles, or in some cases, interconnected squares together into an interlace pattern.

Of course, this sort of Celtic inspiration was actually Germanic in origin some time during the middle Bronze Age but was ultimately adopted by the Celts who carried on the tradition to the point that the style of artwork is associated with them even today.

Clothing

Clothing typically wasn't very varied among the Celts, but there was indication of clothing being used differently by the different casts of society, whether Peasant, Warrior, Priest, or Noble.

Among the Peasants, most of what was worn were wool or linen clothing that was worn in a long sleeved shirt like tunics, with long trousers that covered the legs. Men, and Women both wore these sort of clothing, and it wasn't really uncommon for both to wear pants, as skirts or robes weren't typically seen as a part of the Celtic wardrobe. In fact, skirts and robes were often seen as a Hellenistic custom and were typically eschewed from Celtic culture, being viewed as strange, or Roman-like.

Typically in the Winter seasons though it wasn't uncommon to see cloaks being worn as a way to ward off the cold and kept a Celtic peasant warm, as cloaks were easy to produce, and could be utilized both as clothing to wear, and a blanket to sleep in as well.

When it came to jewelry, though, generally the Nobility were the only ones who held that privilege to wear them, or who could even afford it. Brooches, Armlets, and even Necklaces were generally worn, made of silver or gold and inlaid with precious stones. Though one of the most famous jewelry items that were typically worn was a Torc, which was a thick necklace made of metal and worn much like a collar, with one gemstone or a design that sat in the center of it, resting on the collar.

Sexuality

Pre-Christian society in Europe was dominated by sexual freedom, and the Celts were no different than the other counterparts that had sprung up in Continental Europe in that regard.

In fact, sexuality was viewed as a natural part of life that they generally made no qualms about how it was viewed in their society. It wasn't uncommon for men to take men as lovers, or women to take lovers, and it also wasn't uncommon for married couples to seek out sexual gratification with other people outside of their marriage. To the Celts, marriage was a way of procreation, and to develop an heir line for who inherits what from the older generation. Sex was often viewed as wholly separated from that equation.

In fact, it wasn't uncommon for men to openly prefer male lovers, as typically the Men were separated from the Women in living quarters, and homosexuality was just defined as another part of life. Even Warriors and Druids were expected on some level to have a form of romantic relationship with other men, as it was expected that sexual contact between built stronger bonds between the Warriors and Druids themselves, and homosexuality among women was seen as a way to bond together and a way to expect them to look out for one another. So it wasn't uncommon that Celtic people experimented whenever they can, and differed only slightly more than their historical counterparts at the time.

Chapter 5 – Celtic Religion, Tradition, Spirituality

Tabhair dom Fuaim do mo spiorad Sirona (Give me sound for my spirit, Sirona)

Tabhair dom leigheas do mo spiorad, do mo chroí (Give me healing for my spirit, my heart)

Tabhair dom Fuaim do mo spiorad Sirona (Give me sound for my spirit Sirona)

-Prayer to Sirona, Gaelic Goddess of Healing and Fertility

The Celts were much like any other people during the Late Bronze/Early Iron age people. They viewed the world all around them in terms of a spiritual sense, believing that they were a part of it, and were only separated in the sense that they weren't spiritual beings such as the fairy tales they told of Elves, Trolls, and Goblins, or much like the Gods and Goddesses they worshipped. There was a basic distinction between them, it was believed, but they were still a part of the natural world. What separated them though was that they were mortal beings made of physical substances of the Earth. They were flesh and blood, unlike many of the fairy folks that they developed their mythology around, and weren't powerful enough to influence the material world they lived in, unlike the Gods and Goddesses.

What also majorly separated the Celtic people from their Hellenistic, Nordic, or Germanic counterparts was also their belief in the Otherworld. Their contemporaries at the time believed in an otherworld as well where they would go once they died and passed on, but in other cultures found throughout

Europe, it was believed that their deeds in life carried over ultimately to the afterlife and helped them either achieve peace, or punishment depending on what they did. To the Celts, though, the otherworld was just that. Another world. It was believed by them that the Otherworld was the Home of the Gods and Goddesses they worshiped and that it was a place of Joy where they would be eternally rewarded with feasts, and to live among their ancestors. However, it wasn't heaven as the Celts believed that any and all Celts would go there. Evil people did Evil things in life, true, but to them, it didn't matter as all would eventually pass through. There was no punishment.

Religion

Of course, also like their Hellenistic, Nordic, and Germanic counterparts, the Celts were also polytheistic in that they believed in a varied number of different Gods and Goddesses. Though unlike the other cultures of the time, the Gods and Goddesses that they worshiped varied depending on location, clan, and local flavor. In fact, it wasn't uncommon for one group of Celts to worship a large group of deities, and for a neighboring Clan or group to worship an entirely different group of deities with little to no overlap at all.

It didn't help matters though that the Celts viewed their pantheon differently than the other cultures either. While Hellenistic cultures (such as the greeks) believed the Gods and Goddesses to be all powerful and above humans in every way, and the Nordic cultures believed their gods were separated by different levels of existence through the world tree, the Celts believed that their Gods were very much a part of nature. It wasn't uncommon for them to believe that every tree, bush, rock, flower, or even groups of animals had a deity either among them or living in them. This, of course, led to the belief that each separate deity was either stronger or weaker than other, with some of the deities believed to have been less powerful than humans.

This naturally led to a rather large Pantheon of Gods, where they were separated into General Deities, and Local Deities. Like the words suggest, General Deities were believed to be worshiped on a widespread basis through most of the Celtic culture, dependent on location. Local deities, therefore, were smaller deities that either were among the local nature (Such as waterfalls, or rock formations) or helped protect a clan or even an entire village from danger.

Pantheon of Deities

As was stated, the Celts followed a large number of different deities, and included here in this chapter is just a small sample of the different Gods and Goddesses that they worshiped. Their list of Gods that they worshiped ranged in a large different number, and even what could be classified as a "God" to the Celts varied from Clan to Tribe, to Village or even by different Geographical area. After all the Gaulic tradition of Worship fell more in line with their contemporaries in the area with believing that Gods and Goddesses were above them, while the Gaelic and Welsh Celts believed that Gods and Goddesses were more in tune with the natural world all around them and was just another part of nature. So this list is woefully small.

Gaulish and Brythonic deities

Male

Abandinus, possibly a river-god

Abellio (Abelio, Abelionni), god of apple trees

Alaunus (Fin), god of healing and prophecy

Alisanos (Alisaunus)

Ambisagrus, a god of thunder and lightning, Ancestor God, Sky God, God of Wind, Rain & Hail

Anextiomarus (Anextlomarus, Anextlomara), a protector god

Ankou, a god of death

Atepomarus, a horse god

Arvernus, a tribal god

Arausio, a god of water

Barinthus (Manannán mac Lir), a god of the sea and water

Belatucadros, a god of war

Belenus, a god of healing.

Borvo (Bormo, Bormanus), a god of mineral and hot springs

Borrum, a god of the winds.

Buxenus, a god of box trees

Camulus (Camulus, Camalos), a god of war and sky

Canetonnessis

Cernunnos

Cicolluis god of Celtic army

Cimbrianus

Cissonius (Cisonius, Cesonius), a god of trade

Mars Cnabetius, a god of war[1]

Cocidius, a god of war

Condatis, a god of the confluences of rivers

Contrebis (Contrebis, Contrebus), a god of a city

Dii Casses god of refuse

Dis Pater (Dispater), a god of the underworld

Esus (Hesus)

Fagus, a god of beech trees

Genii Cucullati, Hooded Spirits

Grannus, a god of healing and mineral springs

Intarabus

Iovantucarus, a protector of youth

Latobius[2]

Lenus, a healing god

Leucetios (Leucetius), a god of thunder

Lugus, creation and learning

Luxovius (Luxovius), a god of a city's water

Maponos (Maponus), a god of youth

Mogons (Moguns)

Moritasgus, a healing badger god

Mullo

Nemausus, a god worshipped at Nîmes

Nerius

Nodens (Nudens, Nodons), a god of healing, the sea, hunting and dogs

Ogmios

Robor, a god of oak trees

Rudianos, a god of war

Sedatus[2]

Segomo, a god of war

Smertrios (Smertios, Smertrius), a god of war

Sucellus (Sucellos), a god of love and time

Taranis, a god of thunder

Toutatis (Caturix, Teutates), a tribal god

Tridamos bovine triplication and abundance

Veteris (Vitiris, Vheteris, Huetiris, Hueteris)

Virotutis

Visucius

Vindonnus, a hunting and healing god

Vinotonus

Vosegus, a god of the Vosges Mountains

Female

Abnoba, a goddess of rivers and forests

Adsullata, goddess of the River Savubalabada

Aericura

Agrona, a goddess of war

Ancamna, a water goddess

Ancasta, goddess of the River Itchen

Andarta, a goddess of war

Andraste, goddess of victory

Arduinna, goddess of the Ardennes Forest

Aufaniae

Arnemetia, a water goddess

Artio, goddess of the bear

Aventia

Aveta, a mother goddess, associated with the fresh-water spring at Trier, in what is now Germany

Belisama, a goddess of lakes and rivers, fire, crafts and light, consort of the god Belenus

Brigantia

Britannia, originally a personification of the island, later made into a goddess

Campestres

Clota, patron goddess of the River Clyde

Coventina, goddess of wells and springs

Damara, a fertility goddess

Damona, consort of Apollo Borvo and of Apollo Moritasgus

Dea Matrona, "divine mother goddess" and goddess of the River Marne in Gaul

Dea Sequana, goddess of the River Seine

Debranua, a goddess of speed and fat

Epona, fertility goddess, protector of horses, donkeys, and mules

Erecura, earth goddess

Icaunus, a goddess of a river

Icovellauna, a water goddess

Litavis

Mairiae

Nantosuelta, goddess of nature, the earth, fire, and fertility in Gaul

Nemetona

Ritona (Pritona), goddess of fords

Rosmerta, goddess of fertility and abundance

Sabrina, goddess of the River Severn

Senua

Sequana, goddess of the River Seine

Sirona, goddess of healing and fertility

Suleviae, a triune version of Sulis

Sulis, a solar nourishing, life-giving goddess and an agent of curses

Tamesisaddas, goddess of the River Thames

Verbeia, goddess of the River Wharfe

Welsh deities

Aeron - god of war

Amaethon - god of agriculture

Arawn - king of the otherworld realm of Annwn

Afallach - descendant of Beli Mawr and father of Mabon ap Modron

Beli Mawr - ancestor deity

Bendigeidfran - giant and king of Britain

Culhwch

Dwyfan

Dylan Ail Don

Euroswydd

Gofannon

Gwydion

Gwyddno Garanhir

Gwyn ap Nudd

Hafgan

Lleu Llaw Gyffes

Lludd Llaw Eraint

Llŷr

Mabon

Manawydan

Math fab Mathonwy

Myrddin Wyllt

Nisien and Efnysien (twin brothers)

Pryderi

Pwyll

Taliesin

Ysbaddaden

Female

Arianrhod

Blodeuwedd

Branwen

Ceridwen

Cigfa

Creiddylad

Cyhyraeth

Dôn

Elen

Habondia

Modron, Welsh derivation of Dea Matrona, possible prototype for Morgan le Fay

Olwen

Penarddun

Rhiannon

Gaelic deities

Male

Abarta

Abcán

Abean (Abhean)

Abgatiacus

Aed (Aodh)

Aengus aka Óengus (Aonghus)

Ailill

Alastir

Aí (Aoi)

Balor

Bodb Dearg (Bodhbh Dearg)

Brea

Bres (Breas)

Brian, Iuchar, and Iucharba

Buarainech

Cian

Cichol aka Cíocal

Conand (Conann)

Corb

Credne (Creidhne)

Crom Cruach

Crom Dubh

Dagda aka Dag Dia (Daghdha)

Dáire

Delbáeth (Dealbhaeth)

Dian Cecht

Donn

Ecne

Egobail

Elatha (Ealadha)

Elcmar (Ealcmhar)

Goibniu (Goibhniu)

Lén

Lir

Luchtaine aka Luchta

Lug aka Lugh (Lú)

Mac Cuill, Mac Cecht, and Mac Gréine

Manannán mac Lir

Miach

Midir (Midhir)

Mug Ruith

Nechtan

Neit, Irish god of war, husband of Nemain and/or Badb

Nuada (Nuadha)

Ogma (Oghma)

Seonaidh

Tethra

Tuirenn (Tuireann)

Female

Aibell (Aoibheall)

Aimend

Aífe

Áine

Airmed aka Airmid

Anand aka Anann aka Anu

Badb (Badhbh)

Banba (Banbha)

Bec (Beag)

Bébinn aka Béfind (Bébhinn, Bébhionn or Béfhionn)

Bé Chuille

Beira

Biróg

Boand aka Boann (Bóinn)

Brigit (Brighid or Bríd)

Caer

Caillech (Cailleach)

Canola

Cessair (Ceasair)

Cethlenn (Cethleann)

Clídna (Clíodhna or Clíona)

Crob Derg (Crobh Dearg)

Danand

Danu (Dana)

Ériu (Éire)

Ernmas

Étaín (Éadaoin)

Ethniu (Eithne)

Fand

Finnguala (Fionnghuala or Fionnuala)

Flidais

Fódla (Fódhla)

Lí Ban- (Líban or Liban)

Macha

Medb (Meadhbh or Méabh)

Medb Lethderg (Meadhbh or Méabh Leathdhearg)

Mongfind (Mongfhionn)

Morrígan (Morríghan)

Mór Muman (Mór Mumhan)

Nemain (Nemhain)

Niam (Niamh)

Nic Naomhín

Plor na mBan

Sheela na Gig

Scathach

Tailtiu (Taillte)

Celtiberian deities

Holidays

Festivals, Holidays, or Celebrations were very important to the Celtic people. They lived hard, rough lives tending to farms and fighting off not only the wildlife but each other occasionally. Warfare, survival, and even disease ate away at the little joys that they did have from time to time. So any reason to stop working, celebrate, and come together in the name of peace and joy was especially welcomed among the Celts.

Of course, this led to Festivals and celebrations being some of the more common types of Holiday's that they'd have. Some holidays were spent in quiet contemplation, often spent feasting, and then honoring their Gods and Goddesses, or Clan ancestors. Other holidays were also used as a memorial for important events that happened in their history.

More often than not, though? It was all about the partying. Holidays, Festivals and such were more commonly used as a diplomatic tool to honor and cement a Clan relationships with one another, or to celebrate a Marriage between the young, or to celebrate an especially bountiful harvest.

Whatever the reason though for celebration, you could expect to at least have a fun time. Not only was feasting and relaxing a common thing to experience but drinking Mead (a honey-based beer) was a pastime as well. You could even expect to experience various different games, contests, storytelling, and even music from local bardic talent, and occasionally a fight breaking out or two among bragging Warriors boasting of their skill and abilities.

Chapter 6 – Daily Life of a Celtic Person

"To the brave belong all things." - Motto of the Celts

The daily life of an average Celtic person is pretty much what you would expect from a group of people during the Late Bronze/ Early Iron age. Depending on your status within society, life was pretty average. You woke up, worked, performed your normal duties, and went to bed late at night while doing it all again the following evening.

Of course, this is in stark contrast to the usual stereotype people have of the Celtic people in general. As we've seen throughout the whole book so far, the Celts were anything but their stereotype. Normal conventions and even popular media depict the Celtic people as brutal savages in the dense forests of Ireland or even Scotland who were often naked, armed to the teeth, and viciously assaulting anyone who came into their territory and possibly even flayed their enemies alive, and all sorts of different brutal manners for anyone that wasn't them.

But that's only propaganda that was made by the Romans, and later, the Anglo-Saxons of Britain.

In truth, the Celts were normal in comparison to every other culture in Europe at the time. They predominantly farmed, lived on homesteads in small villages and townships, had a warrior class that watched out for them, and lived like anyone else for several thousand years up until modern times. Though deeply at its roots, they differed with other cultures in several different ways, and the daily lives that they led were different depending on your station in Celtic society.

Here are a few examples of what a typical day in the life of a Celtic person was like depending on their place in society.

Children: Children from a very young age were taught a lot about what it meant to be Celtic. While babies and toddlers were treated as one would expect babies and toddlers to be treated, the moment that a Celtic child grew up and was able to walk, talk and help on the farmstead they were expected to help out at home and even start learning to take a trade. Boys were separated from the girls in gender segregation, where the boys were expected to help their Fathers out in either the field growing food, hunting, or learning basic weapon skills to protect themselves. Girls were expected to remain at home where they were expected to learn how to cook, craft clothing, store food, and handle the business side of running a household that also included the ability to handle finances, despite the Celtic peasant society being based predominately around bartering. At around the age of 15, most children were expected then to think about marriage, and often would meet someone to potentially marry at a local Clan Festival that was located either in their local village, or large township. Usually, also around this age most of the Children were expected to find themselves with a profession. Often the biggest, tallest children were chosen to be specially trained in the arts of warriors, while some would be apprenticed off to learn a trade. Most though would end up becoming farmers, while the girls would be married off to become homemakers.

Men: Peasant men, who weren't of the upper part of society, lived predominately through means of hunting, fishing, and farming. After being married off at around 15-20 years old, it was expected of the young man to either find his own homestead (which was not far from the village) or tend to the homestead of their clan by taking it over from ailing family members. After settling down, and perhaps having children with whom they married life took on a pretty tranquil quality in times of peace. Usually, a Celtic Man was expected to tend to the fields growing various different crops during the Spring and summer months, harvesting what was grown in the Autumn months and preparing it for storage for the coming winter. During the winter, Men were expected to further help stock food supplies through hunting and fishing. If the Celtic Farmer had livestock to raise, they were also expected to take care of the animals as well.

Warriors, on the other hand, lived a vastly different lifestyle than the Peasant. Warriors were expected to be ready to defend their Family first, Clan second, Village Third, and Noble Fourth. Because of this professionalism they didn't learn an art other than the art of combat and were expected to be highly athletic to the point that they constantly trained, and tested themselves in combat. The stronger, and more accomplished the Warrior was, the more honor and prestige was granted to them, with powerful and accomplished Warriors sometimes ascending through the social ladder to either become nobles themselves or even possibly found their own Clan line. So because of this they were constantly prepared to fight and were always training.

Women: Peasant women pretty much lived in the same manner as their Male counterparts, with some differences in how they lived. While the man was expected to do the farming and hunting, Women were expected to remain on the homestead and gather berries, and other various foods in a hunter/gatherer fashion that they would then take what they gathered and share in a collective with the homestead. Usually, though their addition to the homes was in the form of cooking, cleaning, and sewing, often being the ones that would remain at the home and cook for the men and children, as well as keeping the living area's cleaned, as well as learning how to make clothing. A woman who was wed to another Peasant was expected also to help produce children, and keep the family line going as well by helping to create families. While the Women were usually expected to be housewives to the Men and were expected to keep the home, Celtic women differed from other Women in Europe in that they were also expected to know at least some basic level of self-defense skills, often having practiced as children a basic understanding of how to fight with weapons.

Elders: Life for the Celts was very very rough. Warfare, Clan fighting, Honor disputes, and even nature itself in times of peace ensured that the average lifespan of the average Celt was very low. Those that survived past 30 years, or even 40 years were often considered to be "elders" and were revered for having lived that long in a culture that barely survived as is. Elders were seen as resourceful, cunning, and wise and were often the first to be turned to for advice within the village when people needed guidance for anything from home care to diplomatic disputes with their neighbors.

While old age often rendered most elders unable to work, and Elder Warriors were seen as especially favorable, their age, reverence, and guidance often meant that they lived out a comfortable life in their last days.

Conclusion

Thank you again for choosing this book!

I hope this book was able to help you to learn a great deal about the Celts in a short space of time.

Finally, if you enjoyed this book, then I'd like to ask you for a favor, would you be kind enough to leave a review for this book on Amazon? It would be greatly appreciated! Please feel free to give your honest opinions as this could help me make improvements.

Thank you and good luck!

CPSIA information can be obtained at www.ICGtesting.com
Printed in the USA
LVOW10s1429260716

497849LV00035B/528/P